THE REAL ESTATE ESSENTIALS

A Beginner's Guide to Buying, Selling, and Investing

NELLA BYRAN

Copyright

No part of this should be reproduced without the permission of the author.

© Nella Byran 2024

Contents

Introduction 4
Understanding the Basics of real estate 7
Exploring the Real Estate Market 11
Buying Your First Property 15
Financing Options for Real Estate Purchases 19
Navigating the Home Buying Process: From Offer to Closing 24
Understanding Property Valuation and Appraisal 29
Selling Your Property 33
Marketing Strategies for Selling Real Estate 37
Negotiation Techniques for Buyers and Sellers 42
Getting Started 47
Types of Real Estate Investments 52
Managing Tenants and Income 57
Flipping Houses: Strategies for Profitable Ventures 62
Real Estate Investment Trusts (REITs) and Other Investment Vehicles 68
Building Your Real Estate Portfolio: Long-Term Strategies for Success 74
Conclusion 79

Introduction

Real estate is a dynamic and ever-evolving field that offers countless opportunities for individuals looking to build wealth, secure their financial future, or simply find their dream home. Whether you're a first-time homebuyer, a seasoned investor, or someone curious about the intricacies of the real estate market, "Real Estate Essentials: A Beginner's Guide to Buying, Selling, and Investing" serves as your comprehensive roadmap to navigating this complex landscape.

In this book, we'll embark on a journey through the fundamentals of real estate, starting with a solid understanding of its basics. From there, we'll delve into the intricacies of the real estate market, exploring current trends and identifying promising opportunities for both buyers and sellers alike.

Buying your first property can be a daunting task, but fear not—we'll walk you through the essential steps and considerations to ensure a smooth and successful transaction. From securing financing to navigating the home buying process, you'll gain the knowledge and confidence needed to make informed decisions every step of the way.

Understanding property valuation and appraisal is crucial for both buyers and sellers, and we'll cover these topics in detail to empower you with the insights needed to assess a property's worth accurately.

Selling a property can be just as challenging as buying one, but with our expert tips and strategies, you'll learn how to market your property effectively and negotiate the best possible deal.

For those interested in real estate investing, we'll explore various investment vehicles, from rental properties to house flipping to real estate investment trusts (REITs). Whether you're looking to generate passive income or build a long-term investment portfolio, we'll provide you with the tools and knowledge needed to achieve your financial goals.

With each chapter, you'll gain valuable insights and practical advice from industry experts, along with real-life examples and case studies to illustrate key concepts. By the end of this book, you'll be equipped with the knowledge and confidence needed to navigate the world of real estate with ease and success. So, let's embark on this journey together and unlock the potential of real estate investing!

Understanding the Basics of real estate

In the opening chapter of "Real Estate Essentials: A Beginner's Guide to Buying, Selling, and Investing," we delve into the fundamental principles that underpin the world of real estate. Understanding these basics is crucial for anyone looking to navigate the complexities of the market with confidence.

At its core, real estate encompasses land and any structures or natural resources attached to it. This broad definition includes residential homes, commercial properties, vacant land, and even natural resources such as minerals and water rights. Real estate is a tangible asset, meaning it has physical form and can be bought, sold, or leased.

One key concept in real estate is the idea of property rights. Property rights confer legal ownership and control over a piece of real estate, allowing individuals or entities to use, possess, and transfer the property as they see fit. These rights can include the right to occupy, develop, lease, or sell the property, subject to certain legal restrictions and regulations.

Another essential aspect of real estate is its economic characteristics. Real estate is often considered a relatively stable and tangible investment, offering the potential for long-term appreciation and income generation. However, the value of real estate can fluctuate based on various factors, including supply and demand dynamics, economic conditions, and local market trends.

In addition to its economic aspects, real estate also has social and environmental implications. The development and use of real estate can impact communities, ecosystems, and quality of life. As such, real estate development and investment often involve considerations of sustainability, urban planning, and social responsibility.

One of the most important concepts for aspiring real estate investors to understand is the principle of location, location, location. The location of a property can significantly influence its value, desirability, and potential for appreciation. Factors such as proximity to amenities, schools, transportation, and employment centers can all affect the attractiveness of a property to buyers or tenants.

Furthermore, real estate transactions are governed by a complex framework of laws, regulations, and legal principles. These include property law, contract law, zoning ordinances, building codes, and environmental regulations, among others. Understanding these legal aspects is essential for ensuring compliance and mitigating risks in real estate transactions.

In summary, the basics of real estate encompass a broad range of concepts and principles, including property rights, economic characteristics, social and environmental considerations, location factors, and legal regulations. By grasping these fundamentals, aspiring real estate enthusiasts can lay a solid foundation for success in buying, selling, and investing in this dynamic and multifaceted industry.

Exploring the Real Estate Market

In the chapter "Exploring the Real Estate Market: Trends and Opportunities," we embark on a journey through the dynamic landscape of the real estate market, where understanding current trends and identifying emerging opportunities is essential for success.

The real estate market is shaped by a myriad of factors, including economic conditions, demographic trends, technological advancements, and regulatory changes. By exploring these trends, investors and stakeholders can gain valuable insights into where the market is heading and position themselves to capitalize on opportunities.

One key trend in the real estate market is urbanization. As populations continue to grow, particularly in urban areas, there is increasing demand for housing, commercial space, and infrastructure. This trend has led to opportunities in residential development, mixed-use projects, and transit-oriented developments that cater to the needs of urban dwellers.

Technological innovation is also reshaping the real estate market, from the way properties are marketed and transactions are conducted to the design and management of buildings. Advancements in artificial intelligence, virtual reality, and data analytics are empowering real estate professionals to make more informed decisions and enhance the customer experience.

Moreover, sustainability and environmental consciousness are becoming increasingly important considerations in real estate development and investment. Green building practices, energy efficiency measures, and renewable energy solutions are not only environmentally responsible but also economically beneficial, as they can reduce operating costs and enhance property value.

Demographic shifts are another critical factor driving trends in the real estate market. The aging population, for example, has spurred demand for senior housing, healthcare facilities, and age-friendly communities. Meanwhile, millennials are entering the housing market in greater numbers, shaping preferences for urban living, rental housing, and amenities-rich environments.

Furthermore, changes in consumer behavior and lifestyle preferences are influencing the types of properties and amenities that are in demand. From co-working spaces and shared amenities to wellness-oriented design features, real estate developers and investors are adapting to meet the evolving needs of modern occupants.

In exploring these trends and opportunities, it's essential to conduct thorough market research, analyze data, and stay informed about local market dynamics. By staying ahead of the curve and identifying emerging trends early on, real estate professionals can position themselves to capitalize on opportunities and navigate market fluctuations with confidence.

In summary, "Exploring the Real Estate Market: Trends and Opportunities" provides readers with a comprehensive overview of the key factors shaping the real estate market and offers insights into how to identify and capitalize on emerging opportunities. By understanding current trends and staying attuned to market dynamics, investors and stakeholders can make informed decisions and achieve success in the ever-evolving world of real estate.

Buying Your First Property

Buying your first property is an exciting milestone, but it can also be a daunting process. In this chapter, "Buying Your First Property: Essential Steps and Considerations," we'll walk you through the key steps and considerations to help you navigate the home buying journey with confidence.

Assess Your Finances: Before you start searching for a property, it's crucial to assess your financial situation. Determine how much you can afford to spend on a property by taking into account your income, savings, expenses, and any existing debts. Consider getting pre-approved for a mortgage to understand your borrowing capacity and streamline the buying process.

Define Your Needs and Preferences: Identify your priorities and preferences in a property, such as location, size, amenities, and features. Consider factors like proximity to schools, workplaces, transportation, and recreational facilities. Determine whether you're looking for a single-family home, condominium, townhouse, or other types of properties that suit your lifestyle and budget.

Research the Market: Conduct thorough market research to understand current trends, property values, and inventory in your desired location. Explore online listings, attend open houses, and work with a real estate agent to gain insights into the local market dynamics. Pay attention to factors like supply and demand, average days on market, and comparable sales in the area.

Secure Financing: Once you've identified a property you're interested in, it's time to secure financing. Shop around for mortgage lenders and compare rates, terms, and fees to find the best loan option for your needs. Provide the necessary documentation to complete the mortgage application process, including income verification, credit history, and asset statements.

Make an Offer: Work with your real estate agent to prepare and submit a competitive offer on the property. Consider factors like market conditions, comparable sales, and the seller's motivations when determining your offer price. Negotiate terms and contingencies, such as inspection and financing contingencies, to protect your interests during the purchase process.

Conduct Due Diligence: Once your offer is accepted, conduct due diligence to verify the condition and legality of the property. Schedule a home inspection to identify any potential issues or defects that may affect the property's value or safety. Review property disclosures, title reports, and zoning regulations to ensure there are no hidden surprises.

Close the Deal: Work with your lender, real estate agent, and attorney to finalize the purchase agreement and prepare for closing. Arrange for a final walkthrough of the property to ensure it's in the agreed-upon condition. Sign the necessary legal documents, pay closing costs and fees, and complete the transfer of ownership. Congratulations, you're now a homeowner!

Throughout the home buying process, it's essential to stay organized, patient, and proactive in your communication with all parties involved. By following these essential steps and considerations, you'll be well-equipped to navigate the complexities of buying your first property and achieve your homeownership goals.

Financing Options for Real Estate Purchases

"Financing Options for Real Estate Purchases" is a critical aspect of the real estate buying process, as it determines how you'll fund your property acquisition. Let's explore in detail the various financing options available for real estate purchases:

Conventional Loans: Conventional loans are mortgage loans that are not insured or guaranteed by the government. They typically require a down payment of at least 3% to 20% of the property's purchase price and have fixed or adjustable interest rates. Conventional loans are offered by banks, credit unions, and private lenders.

FHA Loans: FHA (Federal Housing Administration) loans are backed by the government and designed to help low-to-moderate income borrowers purchase homes with a lower down payment requirement, usually around 3.5%.

FHA loans have more lenient credit and income requirements than conventional loans, making them accessible to a wider range of borrowers.

VA Loans: VA (Veterans Affairs) loans are available to eligible military service members, veterans, and their spouses. These loans are guaranteed by the Department of Veterans Affairs and offer 100% financing, meaning no down payment is required. VA loans often have competitive interest rates and flexible qualification criteria.

USDA Loans: USDA (United States Department of Agriculture) loans are offered to eligible rural and suburban homebuyers who meet income and property location requirements. These loans provide 100% financing and typically have lower interest rates than conventional loans. USDA loans also offer reduced mortgage insurance premiums.

Adjustable-Rate Mortgages (ARMs): ARMs are mortgage loans with interest rates that can fluctuate over time based on market conditions. They typically start with a fixed-rate introductory period, followed by adjustable rates that can change annually or semi-annually. ARMs can offer lower initial interest rates and monthly payments but come with the risk of rate increases in the future.

Fixed-Rate Mortgages: Fixed-rate mortgages have a constant interest rate and monthly payment throughout the loan term, usually 15 or 30 years. These loans provide stability and predictability, making them a popular choice for homeowners who prefer consistent payments over time. Fixed-rate mortgages are available with various term lengths and down payment options.

Jumbo Loans: Jumbo loans are mortgage loans that exceed the conforming loan limits set by Fannie Mae and Freddie Mac. They are designed for financing high-value properties or homes in expensive real estate markets. Jumbo loans typically require larger down payments and have stricter qualification criteria than conforming loans.

Portfolio Loans: Portfolio loans are mortgage loans held by lenders in their portfolio rather than being sold to investors in the secondary mortgage market. These loans may offer more flexible terms and qualification criteria, making them suitable for borrowers who don't meet conventional loan requirements.

Home Equity Loans and Lines of Credit: Home equity loans and lines of credit allow homeowners to borrow against the equity in their property. These loans can be used for various purposes, such as home improvements, debt consolidation, or major expenses. Home equity loans typically have fixed interest rates and monthly payments, while home equity lines of credit offer a revolving line of credit with variable rates.

Seller Financing: Seller financing, also known as owner financing or seller carryback, occurs when the seller of the property provides financing to the buyer. In this arrangement, the buyer makes payments directly to the seller instead of a traditional lender. Seller financing can be beneficial for buyers who may not qualify for conventional financing or for sellers looking to sell their property quickly.

It's essential to carefully evaluate your financing options and consider factors such as interest rates, loan terms, down payment requirements, and closing costs when choosing the right financing option for your real estate purchase. Consulting with a knowledgeable mortgage lender or financial advisor can help you make an informed decision based on your financial situation and long-term goals.

Navigating the Home Buying Process: From Offer to Closing

Navigating the home buying process from offer to closing involves several crucial steps and considerations. Let's break down each stage in detail:

Making an Offer: Once you've found a property that meets your criteria, you'll work with your real estate agent to draft and submit an offer to the seller. Your offer will include the purchase price, any contingencies (such as a home inspection or financing contingency), and other terms and conditions. The seller may accept, reject, or counter your offer, initiating negotiations until both parties agree on the terms.

Home Inspection: After your offer is accepted, it's essential to schedule a professional home inspection to assess the condition of the property. A qualified inspector will examine the home's structure, systems (such as plumbing, electrical, and HVAC), and major appliances for any defects or issues. Based on the inspection findings, you may negotiate repairs or credits with the seller before proceeding to closing.

Appraisal: Your lender will order an appraisal to determine the fair market value of the property. An appraiser will assess comparable sales in the area and evaluate the property's condition and features to ensure it meets the lender's requirements. If the appraisal comes in lower than the agreed-upon purchase price, you may need to renegotiate with the seller or make up the difference in cash.

Finalizing Financing: While the home is being inspected and appraised, you'll work closely with your mortgage lender to finalize your financing. This involves completing the loan application, providing documentation (such as income verification and bank statements), and satisfying any additional underwriting requirements. Your lender will issue a loan commitment letter once your financing is approved, confirming that you're clear to close.

Title Search and Insurance: A title company will conduct a title search to ensure there are no liens, encumbrances, or ownership disputes associated with the property. Once the title is deemed clear, the title company will issue title insurance to protect you and your lender against any unforeseen title defects. You'll review the title commitment and associated documents to address any issues before closing.

Closing Disclosure: Prior to closing, you'll receive a Closing Disclosure from your lender, detailing the final terms of your loan, including the loan amount, interest rate, closing costs, and other fees. Review the Closing Disclosure carefully to ensure accuracy and clarity. You'll have at least three days to review the document before closing to address any questions or concerns.

Closing Day: On the scheduled closing day, you'll meet with the seller, your real estate agent, and possibly representatives from the title company and lender to sign the necessary legal documents and finalize the transaction. This includes signing the mortgage note, deed of trust, and other closing documents. You'll also pay any remaining closing costs and fees, including the down payment and escrow funds.

Transfer of Ownership: Once all documents are signed, funds are disbursed, and the closing process is complete, ownership of the property will be transferred from the seller to you, the buyer. You'll receive the keys to your new home, and the transaction will be recorded with the appropriate government authority, officially documenting the change in ownership.

Navigating the home buying process requires careful planning, communication, and attention to detail. Working with experienced real estate professionals, such as a knowledgeable real estate agent, mortgage lender, and title company, can help streamline the process and ensure a smooth and successful closing experience.

Understanding Property Valuation and Appraisal

Understanding property valuation and appraisal is crucial when buying or selling real estate, as it provides an objective assessment of a property's worth. Let's delve into the key aspects of property valuation and appraisal:

Definition of Property Valuation: Property valuation refers to the process of determining the fair market value of a property. Fair market value is the price that a willing buyer and a willing seller would agree upon in an arm's length transaction, with neither party being under duress to buy or sell.

Purpose of Property Valuation: Property valuation serves several purposes, including assisting buyers and sellers in determining a property's asking or offer price, helping lenders assess the collateral value of a property for mortgage financing, aiding in property tax assessment, and facilitating estate planning or legal matters.

Methods of Property Valuation

Sales Comparison Approach: This method involves comparing the subject property to similar properties (comparables) that have recently sold in the same area. Adjustments are made for differences in size, condition, amenities, and other factors to arrive at an estimated value.

Income Approach: Commonly used for commercial properties and investment properties, the income approach estimates value based on the property's potential income generation. This method considers factors such as rental income, operating expenses, vacancy rates, and capitalization rates.

Cost Approach: The cost approach calculates value based on the cost to replace or reproduce the property, accounting for depreciation and obsolescence. This method is often used for unique or specialized properties where comparable sales data is limited.

Appraisal Approach: An appraisal is a formal valuation conducted by a licensed or certified appraiser. Appraisers typically use one or more of the above methods, depending on the property type and circumstances, to determine an unbiased opinion of value.

Factors Influencing Property Value: Property value is influenced by various factors, including location, size, condition, age, architectural style, amenities, neighborhood desirability, economic trends, supply and demand dynamics, and environmental factors. Understanding these factors and their impact on value is essential for accurate property valuation.

Appraisal Process: The property appraisal process involves several steps, including property inspection, data collection, market analysis, application of valuation methods, reconciliation of findings, and preparation of the appraisal report. During the inspection, the appraiser evaluates the property's physical characteristics, condition, and improvements, as well as the surrounding neighborhood and market conditions.

Appraisal Report: The final appraisal report documents the appraiser's findings, including the estimated value of the property, the methods used to determine value, descriptions of the property and its improvements, comparable sales data, and any relevant assumptions or limitations. The appraisal report is used by lenders, buyers, sellers, and other parties involved in real estate transactions to make informed decisions.

In summary, property valuation and appraisal are essential processes in real estate transactions, providing objective assessments of a property's worth based on market conditions, comparable sales data, and other relevant factors. By understanding the methods and factors involved in property valuation, buyers, sellers, and lenders can make informed decisions and ensure fair and accurate pricing in real estate transactions.

Selling Your Property

Selling your property can be a complex process, but with careful planning and execution, you can maximize your chances of a successful transaction. Here are some tips to guide you through the selling process:

Firstly, it's crucial to prepare your property for sale. This involves making any necessary repairs or improvements to enhance its appeal to potential buyers. Consider addressing cosmetic issues, such as painting walls, decluttering living spaces, and enhancing curb appeal with landscaping. Staging your home can also make a significant difference by showcasing its best features and helping buyers envision themselves living there.

Next, pricing your property correctly is key to attracting interested buyers. Conducting a comparative market analysis (CMA) can help you determine a competitive listing price based on recent sales of similar properties in your area. Avoid overpricing, as this can deter potential buyers and lead to extended time on the market. Be open to adjusting your price based on feedback from showings and market conditions.

Effective marketing is essential for reaching a broad audience of potential buyers. Work with a real estate agent who can create a comprehensive marketing plan tailored to your property. This may include professional photography, virtual tours, online listings on multiple platforms, print advertising, open houses, and networking with other agents and potential buyers. Utilize social media and other digital channels to showcase your property and generate interest.

When showing your property to prospective buyers, make sure it's clean, well-maintained, and ready for viewing. Highlight its unique features and selling points, such as updated appliances, spacious rooms, or a desirable location. Be flexible with scheduling showings to accommodate buyers' availability and make them feel welcome to explore the property at their own pace.

During negotiations, remain open-minded and willing to negotiate terms with interested buyers. Be prepared to respond to offers in a timely manner and consider factors such as price, contingencies, closing date, and any special requests. Your real estate agent can provide valuable guidance and advocacy throughout the negotiation process to help you achieve the best possible outcome.

Once you've accepted an offer, work closely with your real estate agent and legal counsel to navigate the closing process smoothly. This involves coordinating inspections, appraisals, title searches, and other due diligence activities. Stay organized and responsive to requests from the buyer's lender, title company, and other parties involved in the transaction.

Finally, maintain open communication with all parties involved and be proactive in addressing any issues or concerns that arise during the selling process. By staying informed, responsive, and focused on your goals, you can increase the likelihood of a successful transaction and achieve a favorable outcome when selling your property.

Marketing Strategies for Selling Real Estate

Marketing plays a crucial role in selling real estate, as it helps attract potential buyers and showcase the unique features and benefits of a property. Here are some effective marketing strategies to consider when selling real estate:

Professional Photography and Videography: High-quality photos and videos are essential for making a strong first impression online. Hire a professional photographer to capture your property in its best light, highlighting its key features and selling points. Consider using drone photography to showcase the property's exterior and surrounding neighborhood.

Virtual Tours and 3D Walkthroughs: Interactive virtual tours and 3D walkthroughs allow potential buyers to explore the property from the comfort of their own home. These immersive experiences provide a realistic sense of the property's layout, flow, and design, helping to engage buyers and generate interest.

Online Listings on Multiple Platforms: Ensure your property is listed on popular real estate websites and platforms, such as Zillow, Realtor.com, Trulia, and MLS (Multiple Listing Service). These platforms reach a wide audience of potential buyers and allow them to search for properties based on their specific criteria.

Social Media Marketing: Leverage social media platforms, such as Facebook, Instagram, LinkedIn, and Twitter, to promote your property to a targeted audience. Create visually appealing posts and advertisements showcasing your property's features, amenities, and neighborhood attractions. Engage with followers, share user-generated content, and utilize hashtags to increase visibility.

Email Marketing Campaigns: Build an email list of potential buyers, real estate agents, and industry professionals, and send out regular newsletters and updates showcasing your property listings. Include professional photos, property details, and links to virtual tours or online listings to entice recipients to learn more about your property.

Print Advertising: While online marketing is essential, don't overlook traditional print advertising methods, such as flyers, postcards, brochures, and newspaper ads. Distribute printed materials in strategic locations, such as local coffee shops, community centers, and real estate offices, to reach potential buyers in your target market.

Open Houses and Private Showings: Host open houses and private showings to give potential buyers an opportunity to view the property in person. Stage the home to showcase its best features and create a welcoming atmosphere for visitors. Provide informative brochures or flyers with details about the property and neighborhood.

Collaboration with Real Estate Agents: Partner with experienced real estate agents who have a deep understanding of the local market and a network of potential buyers. Collaborate with agents to promote your property through their marketing channels and facilitate showings and negotiations with interested buyers.

Targeted Marketing Campaigns: Tailor your marketing efforts to specific buyer demographics, interests, and preferences. Consider targeting first-time homebuyers, investors, downsizers, or luxury homebuyers with customized marketing messages and advertising campaigns.

Feedback and Follow-Up: Solicit feedback from potential buyers and real estate agents who have shown the property. Use this feedback to identify areas for improvement and adjust your marketing strategy accordingly. Follow up with interested buyers to answer any questions, address concerns, and encourage them to take the next steps in the buying process.

By implementing a comprehensive marketing strategy that combines online and offline tactics, targeted messaging, and proactive communication, you can effectively showcase your property and attract qualified buyers, ultimately leading to a successful sale.

Negotiation Techniques for Buyers and Sellers

Negotiation is a crucial aspect of the real estate process for both buyers and sellers. Effective negotiation techniques can help you achieve your goals, whether it's securing the best deal as a buyer or maximizing your profit as a seller. Here are some negotiation techniques for buyers and sellers:

Negotiation Techniques for Buyers

Know Your Budget and Limits: Understand your financial situation and set a realistic budget before entering negotiations. Determine the maximum price you're willing to pay for the property and stick to it.

Research Market Conditions: Familiarize yourself with current market conditions, including property values, inventory levels, and average sale prices in your desired area. This information will give you leverage during negotiations and help you make informed decisions.

Identify Your Priorities: Determine your must-have features and priorities in a property, such as location, size, amenities, and condition. Focus on negotiating for the aspects of the property that matter most to you.

Be Prepared to Walk Away: Understand that negotiations may not always result in a deal, and be prepared to walk away if the terms are not favorable. Having alternative options and a willingness to explore other properties can strengthen your position in negotiations.

Present a Strong Offer: Make a competitive offer that demonstrates your seriousness as a buyer. Include any necessary contingencies, such as financing or inspection contingencies, to protect your interests while still appealing to the seller.

Be Flexible and Open-Minded: Approach negotiations with flexibility and a willingness to compromise. Be open to exploring different options and finding creative solutions that meet both your needs and the seller's objectives.

Communicate Effectively: Clearly communicate your expectations, concerns, and preferences to the seller or their agent during negotiations. Maintain a respectful and professional demeanor to foster a positive negotiation atmosphere.

Negotiation Techniques for Sellers

Price Your Property Strategically: Set a competitive listing price based on market conditions, comparable sales data, and your property's unique features and amenities. Avoid overpricing, as it can deter potential buyers and prolong the selling process.

Highlight Your Property's Strengths: Showcase your property's best features and selling points to potential buyers. Emphasize factors such as location, curb appeal, upgrades, and amenities to justify your asking price and attract qualified buyers.

Understand the Buyer's Motivations: Take the time to understand the buyer's motivations, needs, and priorities. This insight can help you tailor your negotiation strategy and identify opportunities for mutual agreement.

Respond Promptly to Offers: Act quickly and decisively when receiving offers from potential buyers. Consider all offers seriously and respond promptly, even if they're below your asking price. Engage in constructive dialogue to explore counteroffers and reach a mutually beneficial agreement.

Be Willing to Negotiate: Approach negotiations with a willingness to negotiate and find common ground with the buyer. Be open to considering reasonable counteroffers and making concessions, such as repairs or closing cost assistance, to facilitate the sale.

Stay Emotionally Detached: Keep emotions in check during negotiations and focus on the facts and objectives at hand. Avoid taking negotiations personally and maintain a professional demeanor to ensure clear and productive communication.

Work with a Skilled Real Estate Agent: Partner with an experienced real estate agent who has strong negotiation skills and a track record of successful transactions. Your agent can provide valuable guidance, advocate on your behalf, and help you navigate negotiations effectively.

By employing these negotiation techniques, both buyers and sellers can navigate the real estate process with confidence and achieve their desired outcomes. Effective negotiation requires preparation, communication, flexibility, and a willingness to find mutually beneficial solutions.

Getting Started

Investing in real estate can be a lucrative way to build wealth and generate passive income over time. If you're considering getting started in real estate investing, here are some essential steps to help you begin your journey:

Educate Yourself: Before diving into real estate investing, take the time to educate yourself about the various investment strategies, market dynamics, and potential risks and rewards involved. There are many resources available, including books, online courses, podcasts, and seminars, that can provide valuable insights and knowledge.

Define Your Investment Goals: Clarify your investment goals and objectives, such as generating rental income, building equity through property appreciation, or diversifying your investment portfolio. Understanding your goals will help guide your investment strategy and decision-making process.

Assess Your Financial Situation: Evaluate your financial situation and determine how much capital you have available to invest in real estate. Consider factors such as your savings, income, credit score, and debt obligations. Determine your risk tolerance and investment timeline to align with your financial goals.

Choose the Right Investment Strategy: There are various investment strategies in real estate, including rental properties, fix-and-flip projects, commercial real estate, real estate investment trusts (REITs), and crowdfunding platforms. Choose a strategy that aligns with your goals, resources, and level of expertise.

Research Local Real Estate Markets: Conduct thorough research on local real estate markets to identify investment opportunities and trends. Analyze factors such as property values, rental demand, vacancy rates, job growth, economic indicators, and demographic trends. Consider working with a local real estate agent or investment advisor for expert insights.

Start Small and Scale Up: As a beginner investor, consider starting small with a single investment property or a small multifamily property, such as a duplex or triplex. This will allow you to gain valuable experience and learn the ropes of real estate investing before scaling up your portfolio.

Secure Financing: Explore financing options for your real estate investment, such as conventional mortgages, FHA loans, private lenders, or hard money loans. Determine the most suitable financing option based on your financial situation, investment strategy, and property type.

Perform Due Diligence: Conduct thorough due diligence on potential investment properties before making a purchase. This includes evaluating the property's condition, analyzing rental income potential, assessing expenses, and conducting a financial analysis to ensure the investment meets your criteria.

Build a Team of Professionals: Surround yourself with a team of experienced professionals, including real estate agents, property managers, contractors, attorneys, and accountants, who can provide valuable advice and support throughout the investment process.

Monitor and Manage Your Investments: Once you've acquired investment properties, actively monitor and manage your investments to ensure they are performing as expected. Implement effective property management strategies, maintain regular communication with tenants, and stay informed about market developments and opportunities.

Continue Learning and Adapting: Real estate investing is a dynamic and evolving field, so continue learning and adapting to stay ahead of the curve. Stay informed about industry trends, regulatory changes, and investment strategies through ongoing education, networking, and professional development.

By following these steps and taking a thoughtful approach to real estate investing, you can lay the foundation for a successful and rewarding investment journey. Remember to be patient, diligent, and proactive in your investment efforts, and seek guidance from experienced professionals as needed.

Types of Real Estate Investments

Real estate offers a wide range of investment opportunities, from residential properties to commercial ventures, each with its own potential benefits and considerations. Here's an overview of the various types of real estate investments:

Residential Real Estate: Residential real estate refers to properties designed for individuals and families to live in. This category includes single-family homes, condominiums, townhouses, duplexes, and multi-family apartment buildings. Residential properties are typically leased to tenants who pay rent to occupy the space. Residential real estate investments offer stable income streams, potential for long-term appreciation, and tax advantages such as depreciation deductions.

Commercial Real Estate: Commercial real estate encompasses properties used for business or commercial purposes. This category includes office buildings, retail centers, industrial warehouses, shopping malls, hotels, and mixed-use developments. Commercial properties are leased to businesses or tenants who operate within the space. Commercial real estate investments can provide higher rental income and potential for appreciation compared to residential properties, but they also carry higher operating costs and vacancy risks.

Industrial Real Estate: Industrial real estate includes properties used for manufacturing, distribution, storage, and logistics operations. This category includes warehouses, distribution centers, manufacturing plants, and industrial parks. Industrial properties are leased to tenants who require space for production, storage, or transportation activities. Industrial real estate investments can offer stable income, long-term lease agreements, and potential for capital appreciation due to increasing demand for logistics and e-commerce facilities.

Retail Real Estate: Retail real estate comprises properties used for retail sales and consumer services. This category includes shopping centers, strip malls, standalone retail stores, and mixed-use developments with retail components. Retail properties are leased to retail tenants who sell goods or services to consumers. Retail real estate investments can provide steady rental income, potential for capital appreciation, and opportunities for value-add strategies such as redevelopment or repositioning.

Hospitality Real Estate: Hospitality real estate includes properties used for lodging, accommodation, and hospitality services. This category includes hotels, resorts, motels, bed and breakfasts, and vacation rentals. Hospitality properties generate revenue from room rentals, food and beverage sales, and ancillary services such as event hosting and leisure activities. Hospitality real estate investments can offer high income potential during peak seasons, but they also face challenges such as seasonality, competition, and operational risks.

Mixed-Use Real Estate: Mixed-use real estate combines two or more types of real estate within a single development or property. This category includes mixed-use buildings, urban developments, and master-planned communities that integrate residential, commercial, retail, and recreational components. Mixed-use properties offer diversification, synergy between different uses, and potential for higher property values and rental income.

Specialized Real Estate: Specialized real estate includes niche or specialized property types that cater to specific industries or sectors. This category includes healthcare facilities (such as hospitals, medical offices, and senior living centers), educational institutions (such as schools and universities), government buildings, data centers, self-storage facilities, and agricultural properties (such as farms and ranches). Specialized real estate investments can offer unique opportunities and income streams but may require specialized knowledge and expertise.

Each type of real estate investment comes with its own set of advantages, risks, and considerations. Investors should carefully evaluate their investment goals, risk tolerance, and market conditions before choosing the most suitable investment strategy and property type. Diversification across different types of real estate investments can help mitigate risks and optimize returns over time.

Managing Tenants and Income

Rental property investing can be a lucrative way to generate passive income and build wealth over time. However, successful rental property management requires effective tenant management and income optimization strategies. Here's how to manage tenants and maximize income from rental properties:

Tenant Screening: Start by implementing a thorough tenant screening process to attract reliable and responsible tenants. This process may include conducting background checks, verifying employment and income, checking rental history and references, and assessing creditworthiness. Screen tenants carefully to minimize the risk of late payments, property damage, or eviction issues.

Clear Lease Agreements: Establish clear and comprehensive lease agreements that outline the terms and conditions of the rental arrangement.

Include details such as rental rates, lease duration, security deposit requirements, pet policies, maintenance responsibilities, and rules for tenant conduct. Ensure tenants understand their rights and obligations under the lease agreement to avoid misunderstandings or disputes later on.

Effective Communication: Maintain open and transparent communication with tenants throughout the rental period. Respond promptly to inquiries, concerns, and maintenance requests to demonstrate your commitment to tenant satisfaction. Establish clear channels of communication, such as phone, email, or an online portal, for tenants to reach you easily.

Regular Property Maintenance: Keep your rental property well-maintained and in good condition to attract and retain quality tenants. Schedule regular inspections and perform necessary repairs and maintenance tasks promptly. Address any maintenance issues promptly to ensure tenant comfort and safety and preserve the property's value over time.

Enforce Lease Policies: Enforce lease policies consistently and fairly to maintain a harmonious landlord-tenant relationship. Address lease violations, such as late rent payments or lease breaches, promptly and in accordance with the terms of the lease agreement. Document all communication and actions taken to ensure legal compliance and protect your rights as a landlord.

Rent Collection Process: Implement an efficient rent collection process to ensure timely payment of rent by tenants. Establish clear rent payment due dates and methods of payment, such as online payments, checks, or direct deposits. Send rent reminders or invoices to tenants in advance of the due date and follow up promptly on any late payments.

Rent Adjustment Strategies: Periodically review rental rates and adjust them in line with market conditions and property value. Conduct market research to assess rental rates for similar properties in the area and adjust your rates accordingly to remain competitive and maximize rental income. Consider offering incentives or discounts for long-term tenants or prompt payment.

Tenant Retention Strategies: Foster a positive tenant experience to encourage tenant retention and minimize turnover. Respond to tenant needs and concerns promptly, address maintenance issues promptly, and provide exceptional customer service. Consider offering lease renewal incentives, such as rent discounts or upgrades, to incentivize tenants to renew their lease agreements.

Property Upgrades and Amenities: Consider investing in property upgrades and amenities to attract and retain quality tenants and maximize rental income. Upgrades such as renovated kitchens or bathrooms, energy-efficient appliances, or modern amenities like a fitness center or community lounge can increase the perceived value of your rental property and justify higher rental rates.

Financial Management and Budgeting: Keep accurate financial records and maintain a detailed budget to track rental income, expenses, and cash flow. Monitor expenses such as property taxes, insurance, maintenance, repairs, and property management fees to ensure they align with your financial goals and objectives. Consider setting aside reserves for unexpected expenses or vacancies to mitigate financial risks.

By implementing these strategies and best practices, you can effectively manage tenants and optimize income from your rental properties. Building positive relationships with tenants, maintaining the property's condition, and implementing sound financial management practices are key to long-term success as a rental property investor.

Flipping Houses: Strategies for Profitable Ventures

Flipping houses, or buying properties with the intention of renovating and reselling them for a profit, can be a lucrative venture if executed strategically. Here are some key strategies for successful house flipping:

Market Research and Analysis: Conduct thorough market research to identify target neighborhoods and properties with strong potential for profit. Analyze local market trends, property values, comparable sales data, and demand for renovated homes in the area. Look for properties in desirable neighborhoods with high resale value and limited competition.

Set a Realistic Budget: Establish a realistic budget for the entire house flipping project, including acquisition costs, renovation expenses, carrying costs (such as mortgage payments, taxes, and utilities), and selling expenses (such as real estate commissions and closing costs). Factor in a contingency fund for unexpected expenses or delays.

Identify Profit Margins: Calculate your desired profit margin for each house flipping project and assess whether the potential profit justifies the investment and effort involved. Aim for a target profit margin that accounts for all expenses and risks associated with the project, typically ranging from 10% to 20% of the property's after-repair value (ARV).

Find Undervalued Properties: Look for distressed or undervalued properties that have the potential for significant improvement and appreciation. Consider foreclosure auctions, bank-owned properties, short sales, estate sales, and distressed sellers as potential sources of discounted properties. Negotiate favorable purchase terms to maximize your profit potential.

Renovation Strategy: Develop a comprehensive renovation strategy to enhance the property's value and appeal while staying within budget and timeframe constraints. Focus on cost-effective improvements that offer the highest return on investment (ROI), such as kitchen and bathroom upgrades, cosmetic enhancements, landscaping, and curb appeal improvements. Prioritize repairs and upgrades that address major issues or add significant value to the property.

Efficient Project Management: Manage the renovation process efficiently to minimize costs, delays, and disruptions. Develop a detailed project plan and timeline, hire reliable contractors and subcontractors, obtain necessary permits and approvals, and oversee the work closely to ensure quality and adherence to budget and schedule. Communicate regularly with the renovation team and address any issues promptly to keep the project on track.

Strategic Marketing and Selling: Develop a strategic marketing plan to attract potential buyers and maximize the property's exposure in the market. Stage the property effectively to showcase its potential and appeal to prospective buyers. Use professional photography, virtual tours, online listings, signage, and open houses to market the property effectively. Price the property competitively to generate interest and offers while still maximizing your profit margin.

Timing and Exit Strategy: Consider market timing and prevailing economic conditions when planning your house flipping projects. Aim to buy properties during market downturns or off-peak seasons when prices may be more negotiable and sell them during periods of high demand and appreciation. Have a clear exit strategy in place, whether it's selling the property quickly for a profit, renting it out for passive income, or holding it for long-term appreciation.

Risk Management: Identify and mitigate potential risks associated with house flipping, such as market fluctuations, renovation delays, cost overruns, and unexpected repairs. Conduct thorough due diligence on each property, obtain proper insurance coverage, and have contingency plans in place to address unforeseen challenges or setbacks.

Continuous Learning and Improvement: Stay informed about industry trends, best practices, and market conditions by networking with other real estate professionals, attending seminars and workshops, and seeking advice from experienced house flippers. Continuously evaluate and refine your house flipping strategies based on feedback, lessons learned, and changing market dynamics to improve your success rate over time.

By implementing these strategies and best practices, you can increase your chances of success and profitability in the competitive field of house flipping. Effective market research, strategic planning, efficient project management, and prudent risk management are key to achieving profitable outcomes and building a successful house flipping business.

Real Estate Investment Trusts (REITs) and Other Investment Vehicles

Real Estate Investment Trusts (REITs) and other investment vehicles offer investors a convenient way to gain exposure to real estate assets without directly owning and managing properties. Here's an overview of REITs and other popular real estate investment vehicles:

Real Estate Investment Trusts (REITs):

REITs are publicly traded companies that own, operate, or finance income-producing real estate across various sectors, including residential, commercial, retail, industrial, and healthcare properties.

REITs provide investors with a way to invest in real estate assets through the purchase of shares or units on stock exchanges, similar to investing in stocks.

REITs are required by law to distribute a significant portion of their taxable income to shareholders in the form of dividends, making them an attractive option for income-seeking investors.

REITs offer diversification, liquidity, transparency, and professional management, allowing investors to access a diversified portfolio of real estate assets without the hassle of property ownership and management.

There are various types of REITs, including equity REITs (which own and operate properties), mortgage REITs (which invest in mortgage-backed securities), and hybrid REITs (which combine elements of both equity and mortgage REITs).

Real Estate Mutual Funds and Exchange-Traded Funds (ETFs)

Real estate mutual funds and ETFs invest in a diversified portfolio of real estate assets, including

REITs, real estate operating companies, and real estate-related securities.

These investment vehicles provide investors with exposure to real estate through a professionally managed fund structure, offering diversification, liquidity, and convenience.

Real estate mutual funds are actively managed by fund managers who select and manage the fund's holdings, while real estate ETFs typically track a specific real estate index and trade on stock exchanges like individual stocks.

Real Estate Limited Partnerships (RELPs)

RELPs are investment partnerships that pool capital from multiple investors to acquire and manage real estate properties or development projects.

In a RELP structure, the general partner (sponsor) manages the investment and makes decisions on behalf of the partnership, while limited partners contribute capital and have limited liability.

RELPs offer tax advantages, potential for passive income, and exposure to specific real estate projects or strategies, but they may involve higher risk and lack liquidity compared to publicly traded REITs and funds.

Private Real Estate Funds

Private real estate funds are pooled investment vehicles that invest in a diversified portfolio of real estate assets, often targeting specific property types, geographic regions, or investment strategies.

These funds are typically open only to accredited investors and institutional investors due to regulatory restrictions and minimum investment requirements.

Private real estate funds offer potential for higher returns, greater control, and access to exclusive investment opportunities, but they may involve higher fees, longer investment horizons, and less liquidity compared to publicly traded REITs and funds.

Real Estate Crowdfunding Platforms

Real estate crowdfunding platforms allow individual investors to invest in real estate projects or properties alongside other investors through online platforms.

These platforms pool capital from multiple investors to fund real estate acquisitions, development projects, or loans, often with lower minimum investment requirements and increased accessibility compared to traditional real estate investments.

Real estate crowdfunding offers potential for diversification, passive income, and access to alternative real estate investments, but it may involve higher risk, limited transparency, and less regulatory oversight compared to publicly traded REITs and funds.

Investors should carefully evaluate the risks, fees, liquidity, and suitability of each investment vehicle based on their investment goals, risk tolerance, and financial situation. Consulting with a financial advisor or real estate professional can help investors make informed decisions and construct a diversified investment portfolio that aligns with their objectives.

Building Your Real Estate Portfolio: Long-Term Strategies for Success

Building a successful real estate portfolio requires careful planning, patience, and a long-term perspective. Here are some strategies for constructing and managing a real estate portfolio for long-term success:

Set Clear Investment Goals: Define your investment objectives, such as wealth accumulation, passive income generation, retirement planning, or portfolio diversification. Establish clear, measurable goals and timelines to guide your investment strategy and decision-making process.

Diversification: Diversify your real estate portfolio across different property types, geographic locations, and investment strategies to mitigate risk and enhance returns. Consider investing in residential, commercial, industrial, and mixed-use properties, as well as diverse markets with varying economic fundamentals and growth potential.

Start Small and Scale Up: Begin with a single investment property or a small portfolio of properties and gradually expand your holdings over time as you gain experience and resources. Reinvest profits from successful investments to acquire additional properties and grow your portfolio systematically.

Focus on Cash Flow: Prioritize investments that generate positive cash flow and consistent rental income to support ongoing expenses, mortgage payments, and portfolio growth. Choose properties with strong rental demand, stable occupancy rates, and favorable rent-to-value ratios to maximize cash flow potential.

Long-Term Appreciation: Seek properties with strong potential for long-term appreciation in value, driven by factors such as population growth, job opportunities, infrastructure development, and economic prosperity. Invest in markets with solid fundamentals and growth prospects to capture capital appreciation over time.

Value-Add Opportunities: Look for value-add opportunities to enhance the value of your properties through strategic renovations, improvements, or repositioning strategies. Identify properties with untapped potential or in need of upgrades that can be leveraged to increase rental income, attract higher-quality tenants, or improve marketability.

Risk Management: Mitigate risk by conducting thorough due diligence on each investment opportunity, including property inspections, financial analysis, market research, and tenant screening. Assess potential risks such as vacancy, market volatility, financing constraints, and regulatory changes, and implement risk mitigation strategies accordingly.

Leverage Financial Tools: Explore financing options such as mortgages, loans, or lines of credit to leverage your capital and acquire properties with limited upfront investment. Use leverage wisely to enhance returns and maximize purchasing power, but avoid excessive debt and maintain adequate liquidity to weather market fluctuations.

Monitor and Adjust: Regularly monitor the performance of your real estate portfolio and make adjustments as needed to align with changing market conditions, economic trends, and investment objectives. Evaluate each property's financial performance, occupancy rates, rental income, and expenses, and adjust your strategy accordingly to optimize returns and mitigate risks.

Seek Professional Guidance: Consider working with experienced real estate professionals, such as real estate agents, property managers, lenders, and financial advisors, who can provide expert guidance, advice, and support throughout the investment process. Leverage their knowledge, expertise, and networks to identify opportunities, navigate challenges, and make informed decisions.

By following these long-term strategies and principles, you can build a resilient and successful real estate portfolio that generates sustainable income, preserves and grows wealth, and achieves your financial goals over time. Stay disciplined, patient, and focused on your objectives, and continue learning and adapting to evolving market conditions to ensure long-term success in real estate investing.

Conclusion

In conclusion, "Real Estate Essentials: A Beginner's Guide to Buying, Selling, and Investing" aims to empower readers with the knowledge, tools, and strategies needed to navigate the complex world of real estate with confidence and success. Throughout this comprehensive guide, we've covered the fundamental principles of real estate, from understanding market trends and property valuation to mastering the art of negotiation and building a diversified investment portfolio.

Whether you're a first-time homebuyer, a seasoned investor, or a savvy entrepreneur, this book provides valuable insights and practical advice to help you achieve your real estate goals. By mastering the essentials of buying, selling, and investing in real estate, you can unlock new opportunities for financial growth, wealth accumulation, and long-term prosperity.

As you embark on your real estate journey, remember that success requires patience, diligence, and continuous learning. Stay informed about market developments, industry trends, and regulatory changes. Adapt your strategies and tactics to evolving market conditions, economic trends, and investment objectives.

Above all, maintain a commitment to integrity, professionalism, and ethical conduct in all your real estate endeavors. Treat clients, tenants, partners, and stakeholders with respect and honesty, and prioritize their best interests at all times.

Whether you're aiming to buy your dream home, sell a property for a profit, or build a diversified real estate portfolio, "Real Estate Essentials" serves as your indispensable guidebook and roadmap to success in the dynamic and rewarding world of real estate.

Thank you for joining us on this journey, and we wish you all the best in your future real estate endeavors. Here's to unlocking the doors to new opportunities and achieving your dreams through the power of real estate.

www.ingramcontent.com/pod-product-compliance
Lightning Source LLC
Chambersburg PA
CBHW070355230526
45471CB00006B/2578